W9-BJQ-896

Swimming Lessons

STONEBRIDGE

Some of the poems included in this collection have previously appeared in:

Fortnight; Books Ireland Review; Bray Arts Journal; Kaleido-scope (Palimpsest Press Canada); *Poetry Ireland Review; Ropes, Stream and Gliding Sun; Broadsheet Series* (Turret Books, UK); *The Burning Bush; The Black Mountain Review; The International Library of Poetry* (USA & UK); *The Shop; The Stinging Fly; The Sunday Tribune; The Cork Literary Review; The Brobdingnagian Times; and The Wildeside Literary Review.*

For their help and encouragement the author wishes to thank John Boland, Anthony Callinan, Carmen Cullen, Mike and Tom Fitzgerald.

For Cathy,
with all best
wishes

Anne Fitzgerald

A. Fitzgerald

Swimming Lessons

STONEBRIDGE

ISBN 1 902410 13 0

Second Impression

Published by
STONEBRIDGE PUBLICATIONS
Ty Beirdd,
53 Church Street,
Ebbw Vale, NP23 6BG.

and

Clifden House,
Corofin,
Co. Clare,
Eire.

Contents

SWIMMING THE CHANNEL

Introduction

The publication of any first volume of poems is a momentous occasion, but all too often, when the first flush of excitement has passed, we find that a poet has no more, or perhaps only very little, to say. Anne Fitzgerald is different. From *Swimming Lessons,* we can be certain that this is, truly, just the beginning. There is a lot more to come.

The poems here are divided into three broad groups, each with its own title; the whole making a cohesive and articulate statement about the development of a very individual poet. At the outset we are pleased to discover hallmarks of real craftsmanship: observation, honesty and wit, and the direct and simple narrative that leaves us wishing that we had said that. Fitzgerald gets there first, every time, as in *Aunts*:

> *'The biscuit tin by the Singer held*
> *a history of buttons and fasteners*
> *that held strangers lives together'*

There is nostalgia too, but not sentimentality. Past events, especially the youthful rites of passage, are remembered matter-of-factly, but with warmth:

> *'...we shed*
> *our childhood like wet togs,*
> *stepping into the warmth*
> *of cigarettes and kisses.'*

As befits a poet whose parents run a public house, the barmaid's eye is keen, her wit is sharp and pointed: *'When pews are traded for bar stools… the snug becomes the true confessional.'* But the observation is not confined to the pub, the beach or the city street. In *Boundaries of a Hinterland*, a man builds a stone wall: *'Stones touch in the knowledge of gaps…A field is enclosed in his stone signature'* Inevitably, one is drawn to make comparisons with Heaney, for the lines are earthy, rooted in the land, in memory and in old bones. It matters little that some of the memories are not her own. She has heard the tales from ageing aunts and grandparents, from old sea-dogs and the occupants of barstools from as far apart as Belfast and Brooklyn. That is *her* living experience and she shares it with us, so that we, like her, may empathise with life as seen and felt by others.

It is from that empathy that so many of the poems here have sprung. In *Harvesting*, where a drunk driver dies, allowing *'the surgeon to harvest the cornea…'.* she refers to the good fortune of a stranger who inherits new sight, but wonders if he might inadvertently inherit *'the night blindness'* of his unfortunate benefactor. In *Missing*, the loss of a child is deduced from a newly-abandoned tricycle. The terror engendered by this awful discovery is referred to simply as a *'statistic'*. It unsettles us, the absence of detail forcing us to think about the event and its consequences in a way that we never do when we read something of the kind in the newspaper or hear it on television or radio.

Throughout all these poems the effect is the same: Fitzgerald displays a deep and sympathetic concern for the plight of Man and the misfortunes that overcome the greatest and the least of the millions who make up that species.

That other poets have been impressed, and more importantly, pleased, by what they have read in this collection is no small matter, for they too have recognised, in Anne Fitzgerald's poems, work of real merit and stature. In that sense, the title *Swimming Lessons* is somewhat misleading, for, knowing Anne's predilection for that most famous of Dublin bathing places, The Forty Foot, which lies in the shadow of Joyce's Tower, I have to say: this lady can *swim*.

Mike Byrne

To my parents
and
Cherry Coogan

'A longing to enquire'

— MATTHEW ARNOLD *The Buried Life*

Paddling

HOME AND AWAY

Where the avenue ends
Howth head stands,
a mountain on the bay,
the lighthouse its guide.

If the lighthouse at Pharos
was the first skyscraper,
then this may be Liberty
and Howth my Manhattan.

There subway steam rises to meet
the mid-day sun. Perfumes waft
me towards Tiffany's while
the homeless find chinks in the light.

To escape the heat I visit
St. Patrick's Cathedral,
where the sanctity of shade
sponges the skin till I'm cool.

Outside by the steps
a hot-dog man stands
where the Vincent de Paul
ought to be.

On the homesick days
I'd go down to the east river
and pretend that Liberty
was the lighthouse at Howth.

Time has framed this view,
yet I will always be a mariner at sea
waiting for the fog to clear
and a beacon to guide me home.

APPLE

From Adam to Newton
you've travelled through
the orchards of time.
Ripe and ready, your stalk
is evidence of our origin.

AUNTS

My father's sisters would mind me
we were a family with an absent
father like the boy from Nazareth.

Kate was the dressmaker who made
my communion frock. Nan taught me
how to laugh and to catch a tune by air.

The biscuit tin by the Singer held
a history of buttons and fasteners
who held strangers lives together:

Worn down with wear, faded by age,
forgotten in the orphanage of shapes.
This is the legacy the seamstress

leaves her niece. Sunlight
turns dust into diamonds
and thorns into a crown.

THE STAMP ALBUM
for Michael Fitzgerald

A brother's gift navigated me dreams beyond oceans,
turning its pages I'd explore new worlds.

Hinging stamps to their alphabetic locations
I become the pilgrim upon this paper highway;

Creating a Baedeker where I am
forever travelling yet never arriving.

Later when I'd visit the real stamp cities
my arrival shatters their distance of a dream.

No warning given for such a journey's end.

FIRST TEACHER

A handful of past pupils
buried Miss Murray,
who for more than half a century

taught the neighbourhood
how to read and write.
Afternoons were the magic

world of colouring pencils.
In practice runs before
our first communion day

she'd give us ice cream
wafers, round as old pennies.
Decimalization reduced

the host along with our
blind belief in what
we can not always see.

Elementary Lessons

In history class I'd journey to Dalkey island leaving
education in the hands of a nun to mould the rest.
Mooring my dreams upon grass and air,

kept watch for Napoleon from the Martello
said mass in a roofless stone church,
no collection basket or musket at hand

only pencil sharpeners and a geometry set;
bouncing sunlight as a hand ball off class room walls
reading my future in the chapters of water.

Twists of poems laid out in the margins of homework.
In the mid-West pupils hide guns in their pencil cases;
handwriting is a dying art in the abattoirs of learning.

ELEPHANT ROCK

for Jennifer Neiland

East of the Forty Foot
rising up from the sea,
is an elephant's head
shaped as a rock.

Barefooted below Joyce's Tower
we'd cross our continent of rock pools
and opportunistic barnacles
to climb our tree house in the waves.

That summer we shed
our childhood like wet togs,
stepping into the warmth
of cigarettes and kisses.

Today that warmth resides in
the new graduates of Elephant Rock,
while our awakenings are memories,
like the emigrating tides who chase

the sunset into the west.

Low Tide

Low tide reveals the beach
to be not a playground
but a furniture showroom.

All race of birds
come to window-shop
through the drapes of the sky.

Rocks are couches with seaweed
for throws, upholstered
with barnacles or laced with algae.

Jellyfish slouch in the sun,
a cobbled pathway
in pursuit of the sea.

So when the waves go out
where do the waves go to?
The some where out there

returns as a watertight cover
to transform this room
into a playground at full tide.

THE DREAM REEL

When day and night fuse
sleep is the source of this voyage.
Without a passport through time zones

I will go. My luggage is memory
whose weight is clarity, releasing the rope
and I'm off on the wave of a dream.

Inside the cinema in my head
I visit with the living and the dead
and new frontiers that I've yet to discover,

like the place between waking and sleeping.
An undercurrent in this dream real
returns me to the pulse of daylight.

Arriving like a foetus from birth
I leave the darkness behind
in the journeys of sleep.

Night Sky

A boy joins dot to dots
creating planets on a page,
where fish swim with dolphins.

Out amongst the blueness
he flies with Pegasus and swans,
closer to the galaxies

than the tree who bore this page.
Touching the embryo of the moon,
he seen that all things connect

to the womb of the sky.
The crayon is the baton
he passes to his children.

INHERITED BELIEFS

Feast of The Assumption, Omagh 1998

A boy plays with Lego and Meccano.
Later he joins the family business

and fights for the cause.
His devotion to metal and plastic

marks atrocities in history.
Strange how toys can surprise.

NOT SO DIFFERENT

for Charles Fitzgerald

Sunday morning before opening time
or pulled pints in my father's pub,
there's an emptiness that fills seats.

I think of another public house
where May goes to pray, Joe to forget.
Both have stained glass windows.

One pays for spirits, the other for belief.
When pews are traded for bar stools,
the snug becomes the true confessional.

Each landlord serves the same parish
with words for poetic porter
and a religious babble for all occasions.

After the first session, dead glasses
on the counter leave a ringed language inside.
Now I see all poems as prayers.

HOME

You and I are the stars
in each other's dreams
snatches and highlights
freeze my nowness.

You disturb my sleep to the point
where I dream with open eyes
stealing my daylight-saving hours.

We are each others life buoy
come home to port, starboard
in one and others breath,
sealed water tight.

LOST AND FOUND
for Leslie Potter

And in a bar in Brooklyn we meet again,
A dry Martini and a Rolling Rock please.

Do you remember this and how I like that
five floors up over a Korean deli, on a bed of ice
watermelons shiver in the sun, traffic shifts gear
Cantaloupes slip, buoyant hulls going nowhere.

We absorb all that is new with a hunger to belong:
its all pastrami on rye, not a Marietta in sight
no squeezing butter between its holes, gold worms
coming up for air, there is none of that over here.

Words are commas in the pauses of our small talk
I give my dry Martini a third olive, a green pyramid in a glass V.
Gin preserves my pursuit for something, altogether elsewhere.
I wait on tables and the day I can say *I made it in Manhattan* —

I spend all my time trying to be someone, somewhere.
On the Staten Island Ferry I say I'm sailing to Howth
in search of a lost race, on Scotsman's Bay Manhattan
looms as Byzantium must have, all those centuries ago.

And with the turn of a head in a crowd or a fragrance
once known grows strong with the scent of memory,
this is what sustains us, when all else lets me down.
No signposts to the land of what ifs, only its own echo
coming up for air, somewhere out there, yet nowhere.

On the way out you throw a few dimes to a down-and-out;
shadows of tug-boats fall, to push our boundaries apart.
A thread comes out of you to the limbo of my soul
a line to the here and now I can grab hold of.
At last, I can remember to forget to remember.

Marietta: a plain thin biscuit
Howth: a headland on the east coast of Ireland, near Dublin
Scotsman's Bay: a bay between Howth and Dunlaoire

*'The human soul resembles water
from heaven it comes, to heaven it goes
and again to the earth, eternally recycled'*

— *Goethe*

Breastroke and Butterfly

WALKING ON WATER

Two granite arms
cut water at Kingstown
and become a pier.

The bandstand
reminds me
of parasol days,

when Irish sweat
hewed granite
from Dalkey quarry;

transported it along
the Atmospheric
Railway line under

English supervision.
Such is the price
we paid for stone.

Now, free, I amble
into the bay
on solid ground.

HARVESTING

for Sinead Fenton

Rain blurs his twenty-twenty vision
swerving to avoid the bend
in the straight white line; darkness holds

barley in memory of one for the road.
Caught in amber an ambulance siren
warns on coming traffic

of broken glass and weather forecasts,
windscreen wipers pendulum on.
Cats eyes guide his remains to theatre.

A generation of strangers inherit
his night blindness
as the eye surgeon harvests his cornea.

HOLYCROSS

for Annie Fitzgerald

This county was divided
into north and south ridings,
a notion from the empire.

My grandmother tells
my mother how we're all
at the mercy of this war.

A foreign luck killed
her husband with a kick
from a horse's shoe.

Black and Tans made free
with widows lands. A knock
at the door would wake

children for generations.
At dawn these men disappear
into the fields with the dew.

JIGSAW

for Medbh MeGuckian

With ten minutes before landing
I look out, Antarctica,
above skyscrapers and icebergs.
No stars but the indigo
of dawn biting into the Turkish
delight of itself:
almost as remarkable as entering
one of your poems.
Earhart in your passport of words
beyond blueness
a continent of promise unearthed.

ACT OF UNION

As the landlord lets new tenants into a yellow room
a partition to create their memories by hand.
How can they know Joe still lives here? He leaves
no loose meat, buttermilk nor *Player's Please*
only a suggestion of ash or dust, or the dust of ash.
He ate news from chips; parcelled papers of yesterday
there are places that claim us and those that warn us away,
in a room where the phone seldom calls out
yet, its light bulb knew no shade.

MOORE STREET

Redundant prams with fruit and veg
draw shoppers down a symphony
of cobbles to purchase more for less,

from the ocean and the earth.
These women are the Wall St. Traders
of their commodities: their hands

are swifter than light and defter
than their closing bell of the dark.
Washed down from a day's gutting

fish scales are stars on the ground.
An abandoned tangerine is the moon
traders leave for the wandering man.

BELFAST REAL ESTATE

And in a glance from a moving train
is a block of flats with its face blown off
bisected by sunlight or not.
Hues of sweets, apricot and lime peel off
walls who housed empires of souvenirs.
Wires and Wavin pipes cut short
behold the hand maiden of the North.

RETURN TICKET

Behind the line before the edge
she sways towards man-made things
a lollipop stick, a compact disk
while half smoked butts smoulder mornings.
In the breeze signalling the trains approach
adrenaline beckons her unmarked stop.

HUNTING GREEN

Dawn plays on marigolds and hedgerow,
after, dew disappears to jump start day.

We drive up a boreen to catch plover off-guard
and hear Matt the thresher from over the yard

whistle Jingle Bells in mid July; thinking of how
his mother would run her index along his larynx,

he rings day-light out of young Martha Ryan.
At the back of an unmarked spot, a twig snaps.

BOUNDARIES OF A HINTERLAND

Accents and rain claim our environs.
A bachelor builds walls
with ancestral hands. Stones touch
in the knowledge of gaps:
of female flesh or of all the children
he might have had. A field
is enclosed in his stone signature.
Weather and trespassers enter,
insects and moss shall inherit
his kingdom of fossils. Speech
from the sky pushes wild violets up.

THE COMFORT OF STRANGERS

At first she writes of hope
here after and weather forecasts.
Then once a month she licks the neck

of his letters, pregnant with blond prairies
swaying under his square of sky.
They met once, to swap vows on death row.

His mind grows slack from years of thinking,
fingering thought as a stone;
the boy in him makes the sign of the cross.

Thunder and lightening open clouds
from Key West to Mizen Head
rain is widespread all over.

Convenience Goods

Seduced by last orders
ankles and high heels
sway into the night.

Married men with wives
who don't understand them
do some late night shopping.

Smoke solicits street corners
bushes become lovers entwined
under a gooseberry moon.

Having purchased under
standing husbands
tuck their daughters in.

Woman with Clipped Wings

I draw the line out on the table top
of the oul lad in the line of my vision:
a part-time craw-thumper and ne'er-do-weller,
tells his gospel of what could have been
to a young wan in a hair band skirt, over
open sandwiches with underrated wines.

By half past two he plunges into his liturgy
for holy hour at the Shelbourne Bar sees
his demons fill seats, in pursuit of sanctuary,
then crown him with his own halo of thorns.

And with the strike of my match he leers
at my orange self-portrait in its tongue

For this young angle I've just happened upon
a Babbycham with a cherry on a cocktail stick

ready to begin again, his game of love.

THE LOCAL EMPORIUM

May comes in of a Sunday afternoon
has her six stout and ten *Sweet Afton,*
Joe's sailed the seas in pursuit of love
in his suit a bit worn with wear, lovely
pair, find anchorage of a kind in Finn's
back bar, on seating sprung with horsehair.

Sun lightens his black stuff, half drunk,
reads its ringed language inside and out,
falls to their floor on all fours:
in search of Venus in their linoleum sea,
with butts for buoys and beer mat boats
Joe's shoes: leather mirrors, a lighthouse of sorts,
his spit and polish takes sunlight out.

In his long white apron and his parish tongue
Ned is Renoir bar man from Horse and Jockey
he's seen kegs of sepia set on Dublin drip trays,
dead glasses and chasers spirit some men away.
His ship's bells rings with Big Ben on de telly.
Joe comes up for last orders, all cheek 'n tongue,

A pint and bottle be the neck, to carry us moonwards…
knocks a whacker back to warm his darkness,
slips coppers into a lifeboat moored at the bar;
fresh mint sinks to sea grass fields where mans'
shadows once trod, on the ship that went down
off the Muglins, full of marble headstones;

Connemara green sailing for Holyhead
algae slabs pave the ocean floor,
sea urchins engrave watermark names.

Time gentlemen please. Have yis no homes to go to?
For God's sake will yis get out, ou' a that…
Out into the night May and Joe go, stars invite them,
frostbitten and brittle waterproof shine dots darkness,
plotting the geometry of a life they might have had.

*'And the gates of it shall not be shut at all
by day, for there shall be no night there'*

— Revelation Ch. 22:25

Swimming the Channel

Uses of Water

Drinking this liquid
we absorb its purity
into our daily Sahara.
It consecrates wine
and cleanses the oasis
of our pleasures.

TRUST

Her skin
is soft
as water
without
ripples
or
exposure
to
sunlight:
she
receives
hailstones
from
heaven
as
gently
as
her
father's
advances.

EARLY ARRIVAL

She swims out
as a swift stone
skimming the sea

beyond starfish
and sea-horses
beyond return.

Forward tides
iron out ebbing
idiosyncrasies.

Garments on a beach
are evidence of her
faithful departure.

MISSING

Wild woodbine and ivy lilies
wallpaper this bike path.

A tricycle lies on its side,
its spinning back wheel beats

time out of still life.
Sweets pattern grass.

Nettles and nowhere are
the tracery of this statistic.

SUNDAY

From a wheelchair she looks out to sea
binoculars in hand and a newspaper on her knee.
She watches a regatta her Cheltenham Gold Cup
blades of colour a rainbow on the flat.
The going is good to fair with furlongs to the horizon
yet, closer than her daughter who wheels her on.

Patterns

'There is no present or no future,
only the past happening,
over and over again, now —'

— Eugene O'Neill
The Moon for the Misbegotten

And by the lighthouse looking out to sea
he watches little sail boats,
colours cast as though a fly fisher is at large.
He was shipbuilder for rockpools,
fashioned hulls from newspapers and shells.

Shadows fall on his shipyard of rocks
as his mother spoons loose tea into a pot
his face darkens under her hand;
so he offers it up with yesterdays news
to stagnant waters bound for distant shores.
Salt will keep her print fresh
and his fingers keen for a face where they'll fit.

MISADVENTURE

'What are they after, our souls, travelling
On rotten brine-soaked timbers
From harbour to harbour?'

— GEORGE SEFERIS *Mythistorema*

Still in the dead of night by the piers' edge,
yes, wind has its way with halyards and stays
plays pussy four corners with yachting masts,
the clink clinking might be ice cubes melting in dry martinis'
on verandas in Killiney Hill, just hours past,
my Almafi, traced by my own naked eye at this dry dock.

Up there we had it all within arm's length
a sea view and nice bits on a mantelpiece
the Mailboat for a clock, the lighthouse a nightlight
one eye on the tides, another on each other,
or so I thought. Seagulls seldom flew this far north
why, for the preservation of their peace of mind.

One day the tide goes out and never comes back
at quite the same angle as before I was let go
to the island in the bay, sporting a barber's pole
up side down cone floats on salt currents
peers into the red and white of sunlight for fear
of voices skimming waves and window pains.

And in the arms of the pier water lays its head
for the night, a bedspread of little sailboats

/...

pattern ripples as a water-colourist might.
Under a new moon cider heads toast stars
I trace the belt of Orion, its red eye puts blood back
in my face as I touch the place where stars are born

and ask the heavens, where do broken hearts go to?
In the wings of moonlight an orange angel waits
— Charon or lifeboat — to rescue me, I am beyond orange,
somewhere over the rainbow in the realm of indigo.
With the foghorn on cue I slip below to catch a falling star
the clink-clinking clinks on and on and on.

DEATH OF A FRIEND SHIP

'A Nymph collected our cares and hung them on trees
A forest of Judas trees'

— GEORGE SEFERIS
Interlude of Joy

Between twilight and night before darkness lands
light throws shapes on shadows, refines outlines.
In the elbows of a pier a banjo player's notes lodge
air pins secrets of its strollers to granite rocks
diamonds glint in my sun slipping into our sea:

a gin and it with a thirst for salt.
It was your -curious way to stop a thought in mid flight
that I saw charm in: a word might hang in the breeze
as mist, to hide the idea behind your thought.

Intrigue lures me into your web of double helix threads
home-made truths spun by your design.
In the small hours the flaws of your ways are at play,

be all about me then on a whim, give me to a dark
acre of your ego, till something better comes along
no Gethsemane or crowing cock all the same.

At night I walk on water
green and red eyes be the end, traffic lights,
traffic lights, I am amber come home to the light

From the pier out across the bay, halos circle ripples
a communion of saints below sea level
a procession of little hulls sailing towards Howth.

Asylum Seekers

At thirty-three Joe practices his scales religiously
fingering ebony and ivory keys as a prayer book;

arpeggios of a childhood in sharps and flats,
with the foot pedals of circumstances he plays

invisible quavers to hear sheet music of a past.
Psychiatrists blame no metronome in the home.

SANCTUARY

At a halting site birds explore debris
clues in pockets of grass; cans devoid of beer,
lost dregs fornicate with the dew.
Even here glaziers have been busy
masking tape secures refuse sacks
to openings blown in by —

And in a pile of rubble lies the crypt
of strangers houses with crisp packets
for stained glass. A shopping trolley
cohabits with blackberry bushes.
Nettles and dandelions secret
a concrete pipe, a home from home

for a runaway boy who finds comfort
of a kind in dog-leaves and weeds.
Who would have thought bluebells could
exist amongst a skip and a satellite dish.
The pavilions of this wasteland cherish
his dreams in a way his mother should.

The larcenist of his days was her Oedipus
complex. Forget-me-nots whisper no
sweet nothings to his wanderlust.
Psychosis is his kingdom, come
what Mai, a family that plays together
stays to get her, home sweet home.

OUT OF THIS WORLD

'From the deceits of the world,
the flesh and the devil
good Lord, deliver us'

— THE BOOK OF COMMON PRAYER

We drive off the beaten track with a throw away remark
to where colour bends danger
orange burnt in memory of maroon.

Sunlight reaches dark cornered thoughts
our speech lies hidden in stops and starts
in the days when a look said it all.

Instead of malt whiskey or creamed tea
you take to me when your other half leaves.
You step into the cold baths that I leave

to save the water is what you always say
winking back at stars down the drain:
you pull the plug to know the cord's not cut.

I sit in his place I become him through you
with you in me mind's gone for its tea
all glory and honour is yours almighty father.

Back on the dual carriage way I go in on myself
like the twist of a song longing to be sung:
somewhere between the Gods and the Mailboat

A mother's love a blessing no matter where you roam,
it was in your nature to possess no St. Christopher
save for the Christ you made of me dear mother of peril.

No True Road

Driving into the darkness before dawn
a half moon hangs as a holy picture might
above a crescent of semi-detached homes.

Behind the facade of number twenty-eight
Pandora's box flourishes as a corn beneath skin
the poultice of a stranger draws the white I out:
paternal root of all evil and mother of invention
hinders the gait of their thirty-three year old boy.

By the age of seven they take his reason
over humped backed bridges into their by-ways
not marked on his minds' map, circling roundabouts
as the revolving door of the Shelbourne. A toy
of their own for all seasons, for no particular reason.

Dead to the world the moon makes Lazarus of him
jiving with his self-portrait in the orange sky light:

I am a child of the street, cut out of my whereabouts
I am a shadow in doorways with a cup in my hand
I am a man in the church who prays to false Gods
I am the child of Prague with a collar of parental glue
so, who is the Madonna who holds the lost child in me?
I am the boy next door, the man in a car who overtakes
and no speed limits apply in the highway of my mind
road works ahead always road works a head of me.

A miraculous medal hangs from his inside mirror
half truths and white lies blacken his tongue
with the ease of air brightening blood.

No nuns or nurses in white shoes legging it over
man-made squares only cowslips and thistles on vigil
a breeze of no fixed abode follows his lunar stride.

Remote Control

— F. Scott Fitzgerald
The Great Gatsby

And something gave way like the snap of a twig
changing the ground beneath my feet forever,
the indisputable privacy of the mind.
Unaided by white sticks blind eyes are the weapons of guilt
and secrets the toxins of the mind. Open wounds,
a regatta of emotions moored to another's darker sails.
Parental hulls cut water creating silent ripples
amongst the waves of their entails.
Meteorologists gave no warning,
yet, hindsight fashions evidence of the perfect water jig saw.
The third eye saw this storm in technicolor,
now with the gentleness of an old movie
the Redemptive Father's salvage of a shipwreck begins.
Past the granite and glass, plants boldly exist
in a could be lounge-bar, circa 1970's.
In the absence of flock wallpaper stale smoke traces
a hinterland of past patients, whose alumni is John of God's.
Their demons ingrained in walls, re-ignited with the strike
of each new match burning four inches of a past.
How idiosyncrasies betray us, amplifying our weaknesses.
The alcoholic drinks mineral water in memory of whiskey,
barley matured from a casket of earth, not oak.
Time is measured by moving his spiritless glass
in small circles over an invisible beer mat;

by the close of visiting hours ash hills of sorrow crowd
his saucer as each dead butt becomes someone who forgot.
For our brief sojourn we call this place circuit land
green acreage that property developers would die for,
a Pride and Prejudice set, two sage bushes remain
from an imaginary maze.
A perimeter of trees strategically planted to shake
the shambles from inmate's limbs, their arms hang down,
heads crucified by their structure, shadows navigate
their way in the noon day sun
as they learn to remember how to walk on the inside out.

Behind the granite and the glass again,
my imagination takes sunlight by the hand, true companions
voyaging into the sea grass fields of circuit lands' maze
Narcissus rises from a shucked oyster shell
casting pearls before swine, sequenced swimmers clock time.
Raleigh rolls cigar leaves with paedophiles
a braille water-colourist reads the sky with Michangelo,
scorched white clouds ribbed across the great abyss.
Pythagoras finds the right angle: remote control,
the sum of the squares of parental sides, obtuse heirlooms
for their Pavlovian children, triangulating a man into a boy.
Hermes hears Judas whisper at sunset
Janus lets Garbo in, leaving the moon out
guiding Odysseus home.
I walked the corridor's square straight line
like a child avoiding pavement cracks.
As discharge beckons journeys end

I begin to weave a little and wonder:
where is the line that draws some in
as I out pause Beckett?

Unmooring an undercurrent somewhere out there
in the nowhere of my mind.
Perhaps visiting leaves me with a want
in the visited to cast a lifebuoy out to all adrift.
In the backwash I see the last frontier
as Old Moore's Almanac can not.
In giving I lose a part of myself,
remaining days are spent piecing the bits back
perhaps it is the voyage for my own watermark
in another, the perfect water jig saw.
I believe in the existence of lighthouses
in parental sirens waving from a pier,
in the lifting of fog and that
triangulating sails journey the tides
waiting for a beacon to guide them home.